VIA FOLIOS 55

Italici

Italici

An Encounter with
Piero Bassetti

by
Paolino Accolla
Niccolò d'Aquino

BORDIGHERA PRESS

Library of Congress Control Number: 2008939539

Originally published in Italian by
Giampiero Casagrande

Incontro con Piero Bassetti

English translation by Robert Brodie Booth

Cover photo: Luca Fantini

Printed in the United States.

Published by
BORDIGHERA PRESS
John D. Calandra Italian American Institute
25 West 43rd Street, 17th Floor
New York, NY 10036

VIA FOLIOS 55
ISBN 1-59954-001-0

PUBLISHER'S NOTE

We are delighted to be able to publish Piero Bassetti's *Incontro*, what we see as a most significant "conversation," in English. We use such a term here in our opening comments because of its etymology, from *cum-* and *vertare*. In its original meaning of "having dealings with others," also "manner of conducting oneself in the world," as we read in most dictionaries, there is indeed need of a new conversation in the world.

Much has taken place in the past two decades in Italy, both socially and politically. From *Mani Pulite* to the dissolution of some parties and the creation of others, from Italy becoming now a country of arrival as opposed to its historical posture as one of departure, a new discourse and its attendant vocabulary prove to be an invaluable addition to this new era of the "Post-Italian," as Bassetti tells us in the pages that follow.

We have surely witnessed a certain expansion of geopolitical boundaries with regard to Italy and its citizenry. Such a process has it roots in a plethora of enduring sociopolitical events, be they the historical emigration that began in the nineteenth century, be they the more recent laws of the vote abroad or the acquisition of Italian citizenship to progeny of those immigrants who first confronted challenges of the migratory act.

This combination of a physical and virtual expansion proves to be the latest in developments that fall under that far-reaching umbrella we characterize with the adjective Italian.

The Editors
BORDIGHERA PRESS

PREFACE

The English translation of *Italici* is the fruit of a fortunate encounter between the Italian/American Digital Project and that side of Piero Bassetti's multifaceted personality that led to the foundation of *Globus et Locus* ten years ago.

A few months ago Bassetti—a renowned entrepreneur, politician, and a public intellectual—invited us to the headquarters of Globus et Locus in Milan, after discovering i-Italy.org on the Web. There, we had a rich exchange of opinions on what turned out to be a mission we deeply share: the creation of a virtual network for "Italic encounters."

He told us that he had been waiting for years to assist in the spontaneous creation "from the bottom" of the first nodes of that network, and singled out i-Italy.org as one of them. We were flattered by his appreciation: we were aware that Piero Bassetti had been working for years on the theme of *Italicity*. We also knew that he approaches it in a provocative way—outside of the classical schemes, relieved from the inflated registers sometimes utilized in institutional discourse, and also from the most common stereotypes.

As editors of i-Italy, we are aware that the creation of an authoritative point of encounter, information and communication on the Web for the *Italic* community is not only possible, but it is a strongly-felt necessity. Together with our bloggers, readers, and online community members we have been working at this for over a year in order to lay the first bricks of the kind of *Italy-city* this book proposes. This is why, brief but incisive as it is, this book immediately caught our attention.

True, when we offered to explore the possibility to publish it in English, we already knew we had a good chance: we were certain that the most authoritative member and co-founder of the Italian/American Digital Project, Anthony Julian Tamburri, Dean of CUNY's John D. Calandra Italian American Institute and co-director of the Bordighera Press with Fred Gardaphé and Paolo Giordano, would be enthusiastic about it. The Italian/American cultural community, which has provided inspiration and support to many of our initiatives, seemed the perfect environment to start this dialogue.

We turned out to be right, and thus the book you hold in your hands now is the product of just two months of intense collaboration with Piero Bassetti — via the Internet, of course.

We invite the native English reader — who will find him- or herself to be an "Italic" right from the very first pages — to approach this book not as a plea for the revival of some sort of exclusive sense of ethnic belonging, but rather as a sort of textbook for the cosmopolitan Italic citizen of the third millennium, one who feels his to be part of a constantly growing network of multiple, intertwined, *g-local* identities.

Letizia Airos Soria
EXECUTIVE EDITOR, I-ITALY.ORG
THE ITALIAN/AMERICAN DIGITAL PROJECT

CONTENTS

9   A Conversation on *Italici*
     Piero Bassetti

11   A Summer Revelation on the Appia Pignatelli
     Niccolò d'Aquino

21   The Long Story of a Contemporary Idea
     A Conversation with Piero Bassetti

49   Explanations and Interstitial Musings

65   The Glocalist Manifesto
     Piero Bassetti

67   Italian Publisher's Thoughts

68   We Are Glocalists . . .

75   The Authors

77   Globus et Locus

A CONVERSATION ON *ITALICITY*

by Piero Bassetti

I am delighted to contribute a brief introduction to this book that, thanks also to Paolino Accolla and Niccolò d'Aquino, with whom I enjoyed a fertile and lively cultural exchange, brings to the public's attention the very relevant theme of *Italicity*. I was only too pleased to be involved in this conversation because I believe it is a subject that should reach a wider audience. *Italici* and *Italicity* are recognized, lived and, not to be underestimated, "imitated" throughout the world: the networks of Italic contacts and organizations acquire depth and awareness, and *Italicity* is beginning to be seen as the "future destiny" of a community of great global importance.

However, the *Italici* community, despite its undoubted reality and popular importance, has not yet been given its fair due by the media. To make up for this deficiency, this book highlights all things *Italic* that today need to be restored to a dimension worthy of their supranational value. *Italicity* goes beyond the already significant *Made in Italy* and feeds off the culture and values of some 250 million people who, in a very *Italic* way, live and breathe the globalized world and the *mobile present*.

This book is the result of our conversation. I am extremely satisfied with it. However, I know that the reader's opinion is the one that really counts.

A Summer Revelation on the Appia Pignatelli

by Niccolò d'Aquino

The year was 1993. The offices of a Milanese financial weekly. Quite by chance, an invitation, lying forgotten on an editorial secretary's desk, caught a reporter's eye. It told of a meeting to be held by an organization he had never heard of: the Association of Italy's overseas Chambers of Commerce. It was the beginning of summer, a time notoriously void of news. Caught off guard, the chief editor shrugged: "If it means that much to you, go see what it's all about."

The meeting, or rather the convention, was in Rome. At the Tagliacarne Institute, a magnificent building immersed in the lush green of the Appia Pignatelli. However, it was not the pleasant architectural lines that caught the reporter's eye. It was not even the quite surprising discovery that the sixty or so overseas Italian Chambers of Commerce took care of more than 20,000 companies, big and small, spread around the world: a network of extraordinary potential that, at the time, was barely known to the newspapers, even the financial ones. No, what really raised the stakes were the speeches, many of the topics totally alien. Others, on the other hand, dealt with familiar subjects — *Made in Italy*, the problems of Italian entrepreneurs around the world, the Italian government's indifference to any and all political dealings with those who worked abroad. But, even the more widely known problems were dealt differently. For once, the view was not Italocentric and institutional, nor was it from the Farnesina or the Ministry of Foreign Affairs, in other words from the Rome government.

Secretaries, chairmen and CCIE—Camere di Commercio Italiane all'Estero (Chambers of Italian Commerce Abroad)—executives spoke with the expertise and familiarity of those who had lived overseas for a long time. They voiced their concerns, both common and specific. But always packed with facts and data, the unmistakable result of a true awareness of the relevant matter and with a solid footing in the territory.

Once over the initial amazement and having assimilated this hitherto unknown information, what really struck the reporter was the fact that everyone—both on the stage and in the audience—spoke Italian. The Italian language was spoken with the most diverse accents and inflections: from French to German, from British English to American and Australian English, from Spanish Castilian to Argentine Castilian. The speaker entrepreneurs and executives all had Italian surnames: Pallaro, Turano, Pollastri, and many more originating from the *Belpaese* (the Beautiful Country as Italy is often nicknamed by Italians). The years lived abroad, in many cases a single generation, but often more, have left their mark.

There were more than one hundred international operators at the Tagliacarne that day, businessmen from all over the world, all packed into that hall, discussing, arguing. And all using Italian as the common language. Which, for the first time, proved to be a business Esperanto, an alternative to the customary *business English*. That Roman summer day saw the forceful emergence of *another* Italian language. Different from the language belonging to what was once considered a minority on the verge of extinction, only good for a snobbish and decadent code applicable to international and sophisticated niches: opera aficionados, refined art lovers, well-read men and women with Renaissance or Dantesque passions. Different from the Vatican Esperanto, the *language* of bishops and priests spoken at even the most remote missions. Or the abbreviated version spoken by the overpaid players of the football jet set.

The convention was chaired by Piero Bassetti, the only celebrity present. It was his name that tore a reluctant "okay" from the Milanese chief editor, thus giving the reporter the go-ahead for his Roman trip. From the world of Milanese entrepreneurs and a qualified economist, but with a passion for politics, Bassetti was the first president of the Lombardy region. Then, elected to Parliament, he did something unusual: he renounced all parliamentary rights, and resigned voluntarily. Not everyone understood his reasons, the truth being he did not like the Roman political atmosphere. Choosing the world of economics and called to run Milan's powerful Chamber of Commerce, Bassetti was at the Tagliacarne Institute that day as the freshly appointed chairman of the overseas Chambers of Commerce. It is the association—the umbrella organization wanted by him and created in 1987 to coordinate the activities of some sixty overseas Italian Chambers—that he only took charge of in 1993. He was the only one to speak a new language: "metanation," "global tribes," "bottom-up aggregation." Not once did a simple term like "emigration" escape his lips. He insisted on using the word "Diaspora." The reporter picked up on the grumblings and arched eyebrows around the hall. Right. From Los Angeles to Sydney, from Frankfurt to Cape Town, the Italian entrepreneur does not feel he is part of a *Diaspora*, the word more often than not associated with the mass dispersion of peoples escaping religious or racial persecution. It will take years before the spread of Italians around the world will be accepted in a Bassettian way of thinking as a *Diaspora*—first, workers emigrating with few or no professional skills, then managers of increasingly higher qualifications. A phenomenon that in time, Bassetti still insists, took on a marked political tilt. From both the directly interested and Rome's central institutions, the reactions to the political project of a Diaspora capable of serving behind the scenes and as the foundation for an Italian business community abroad will be cold, to say the least. It will take years to make people understand that the figures of this phenomenon have nothing to do with the conservative figures found in official bureaucratic lists: between three to five million Italians are registered with AIRE, the directory of Italians living abroad. And that is official. But what about the sixty-five million emigrants and their children? They do not count!

Until that date, the basic view, corroborated mostly by Italian politics — with a few praiseworthy exceptions, especially from the right — was that the "Italian Italian" had turned his back on his emigrated relatives. Given up for dead, lost. Total strangers. Perhaps even ashamed of that cardboard suitcase shut with string. Blood relatives to be disregarded. To be reinstated only in the event of a highly improbable, totally unexpected inheritance from some American uncle.

Instead, taking note and starting from this feeling of extraneousness — a mutual sentiment, expressed with rancor by that *Italian outside Italy* — Bassetti suggests, as a first stage, a systematic verification of the entrepreneurial dimensions of the Italian *Diaspora* in the world. The objective being to find ways and time for the aggregation that was requested haphazardly by increasingly more parties. Though unknown by most, a new process *perceived* by Bassetti had taken off. The traumatic schism caused by the mass emigration of the late nineteenth and early twentieth centuries was beginning to mend: the "new" homeland seen by most as the only homeland, if for no other reason than a source of income; the "old" one only good for a visit or simple nostalgia. One could determine the parameters of a social revival capable of exerting a powerful force of aggregation, along with a desire and a sense of redemption.

Like Saint Paul on the road to Damascus, the reporter, who had happened upon the invitation to the Tagliacarne Institute by pure chance, and who is now writing these words, was stunned and won over. He approached Bassetti, and spoke to the representatives of the overseas Italian Chambers of Commerce. Hence, the beginning of a collaboration. The following year (1994) saw the publication of *I media della diaspora*,[1] in the conviction that communication and information were the more neutral and less intrusive basic binders of any network. That first systematic cataloguing of the vast but irregular and ignored universe of small and very small newspapers, publications and reports, and the radio and TV programs of the countless Italian communities spread across the five continents, brought it all to an extraordinary conclusion. Media that, taken by themselves, boast minimum numbers. But, put together, amount to over four hundred publications. With an overall circulation of more than a hundred million copies. Figures that, ten years later, will be substantiated and amplified by two more in-depth studies.[2] Thus confirming a staggering picture. The new calculation shows that there are at least 679 publications dedicated to Italy, perhaps not printed in Italian, but in the language of the local community. The Internet webs are countless, and growing in numbers, difficult to keep tabs on. As far as radio and TV programs are concerned, they transmit over 140,000 hours annually. While the census dealing with communicators, the operators of information and of publishing, ascribed in some way to what will soon be called *Italicity*, figure 1,400.

---

[1] Niccolò d'Aquino, *I media della diaspora: giornali, radio e televisioni fuori d'Italia*, preface by Piero Bassetti and Susanna Agnelli, Minster of Italian Foreign Affairs. Rome: Department of Information and Publishing Editions, 1994.
[2] Margherita Peracchino, *Yearbook of the Italic Mass Media in the World*, and *Yearbook of Italic Communicators in the World*, preface by Piero Bassetti, Lorenzo Del Boca, Niccolò d'Aquino. Turin: MediaPress, 2004.

Intellectually, the Bassettian project enjoyed its first scientific verification in 1995. *Il Mondo in Italiano* (The World in Italian),[3] a work by two sociologists, Consuelo Corradi and Enrico Pozzi, throws light on the accumulation of interests, and the links between relationships and culture that unify a major part of the sixty-five million Italians living abroad. A link that often exists without their knowledge, and is frequently, if not always, rejected.

Suspicion and resistance, after all, are the constant reactions to Bassettian thoughts and projects. The strategic values of the Italian nature and the network that binds it are nearly always rejected with an ironic smile and a shrug. Very few believe in the "great extended and open community that, over the past few years, has reinforced its global penetration and presence in an extraordinary manner," as Bassetti says. It is not easy to accept the emergence of "a virtual community not modeled on traditional criteria of identification and association; capable, however, of growing stronger and stronger, in such a way it knows how to open up and make itself available to new and continuous support from abroad, how to constitute a network of well connected poles, even without territorial continuity."[4]

The current idea of a national or ethnic global network is accepted by politicians, scholars, and journalists only if it is a network or commonwealth like that of the Anglo-Saxons, Spanish and, more recently, Chinese. It seems difficult for some to understand that the same connections that, for example, link the Chinatowns of the world or Anglo-American *businesses* are also at the base of the Italian *business community*, although more subterranean and — as we say — often denied. There is indeed a globalization that speaks Italian, too.

---

[3] Consuelo Corradi and Enrico Pozzi, *The World In Italian. The Italians in the World between Diaspora, Business Community and Nation*, preface by Piero Bassetti. Milan: The Exercise Book of Business and State, the Milan Chamber of Commerce, 1995.
[4] Piero Bassetti, "The World In Italian," *Limes* 4 (1998).

Difficult, but not impossible. Over the years, it has been the evolution of the globalization process that supplies the instruments to help understand, to rid the most suspicious of their doubts. The second part of the nineties saw the surpassing of globalization, of the discovery of "global and local" and, at the same time, the so-called *glocal*. The local reacts by watching the global horizon. Or rather, the affirmation of an added value, particular every time because every subject and community is particular. A necessary and welcome development of that phenomenon — globalization — that at first appeared simply to want to frame the world in a single system, eliminating every difference. A reassuring response to the anxieties that mass internationalization — seen and feared as being reliant on and culturally and economically colonized by the dominating American model — triggered in a major proportion of the world's public opinions. With numerous *non-global* setbacks, of an inherently conservative nature, amongst the more liberal of the world's population.

It is the idea of *glocal* — think globally, act locally — that acts as the foundation to the developments of Bassetti's deliberation, which, and it goes without saying, creates even more suspicion. Also, because the next step — following the birth in 1997 of Globus et Locus, a sort of think tank in which Bassetti involves territorial, banking and academic institutions — leads to the singling out of a brand new global typology — the Italici.

And it is here that an already experimented problem pops up again. Just as happened years before with *Diaspora*, the term *Italico* is struggling just as hard to be accepted. Who are the *Italici*? Yes, they are also Italians, of course. Better still: Post-Italians. Of Italian extraction, but also Italian-speaking, Italianists, Italophiles. Citizens of Italian-speaking nations and regions: Italian Switzerland, Dalmatia, Istria, San Marino, Malta. And then there are those men and women who, though they do not have a single drop of Italian blood in them, share the same values and style of life, the unmistakable models of that *Italian way of life* that the expansion of the Italian economy has, over the past few years, spread around the world. The young and not so young who have chosen that particular style amongst the many put on offer by the wares of international industry. And let us not forget the managers and entrepreneurs who base their professional activities on the products and initiatives linked to Italy or to products of an Italian flavor. So the figures and numbers change. Or rather explode. One can count on about two hundred million people spread over the five continents.

Between the end of the nineties and the start of the twenty-first century — after years and years of talk, arguments, empty promises — Rome finally gave the Italians living abroad the right to vote. But it has not been that straightforward, confusion still reigns, and all sorts of problems have arisen.

For Bassetti, the perennial, far-seeing rebel, this is the season during which, along with seminars, conferences, publications, and new websites, the *Italici* Project kicks off: the transnational gathering of the circa two hundred million men and women who, unbeknownst even to themselves, are "likely to take on a serious political importance."[5] Taking advantage of the experience and lessons learned at the birth of the overseas network of Italian Chambers of Commerce that are, and intend to remain as such, associations of *Italic* inclination, of great local interest: the Buenos Aires Chamber is Argentine, the Caracas one is Venezuelan, and so on and so forth. Or rather, in the *glocal* era, the global aggregation, the birth and the development of a global network or, if one prefers, of an *Italic* commonwealth must have a bottom-up future, respecting freedom and territorial tendencies.

---

[5] Sergej Roiç, *The Italicity Route.* Milan–Lugano: Globus et Locus and Giampiero Casagrande Publisher, 2006.

Certainly: "This movement, or transnational community, born and raised within a vast global Diaspora, has become a serious aggregation of people from all walks of life, united by the same values, culture and common interests, still in need of growing with regard to self-awareness, to knowing where they belong, where they came from—but no less important and demanding—to then emerge and develop from a Media point of view" (Roiç).

And it is with this in mind that the *Italici* Project took off. The next step will be the creation of a multimedia platform, in line with the inhabitants of this global village, united on the web and in line with the universal spirit of the heirs to this culture of humanism.

The *Italicity* platform is a permanent *work in progress*. It will be a place and a meeting point for the planet's two hundred million inhabitants who live according to values honed and consolidated over centuries of *civitas italica*. They are not simply shared (and shareable) values. They are also the driving force behind new beginnings, of communal life, not all currently imaginable. *Italicity* is a political alchemies' instrument of precipitation for years to come. It is the place of the Media, which in our time means place of *polis*, where meditation is replaced by immediacy. It is, therefore, a second life. An open place where every creation, project, and scenario may experiment and verify its own feasibility.

The coming years will tell us whether or not this is a possible dream.

The Long Story
of a Contemporary Idea

A Conversation with
Piero Bassetti

.

❖ *Italicity and Italici: these words are beginning to make inroads into our everyday language. But how did you intuit this new form of Italianity that is spreading across the globe? When did you first "suspect" that a potential network of Italianity existed in the world?*

My first "suspicions" surfaced when I became President of the Chamber of Commerce at the end of the eighties, and subsequently learned of the overseas Italian Chambers of Commerce. I immediately understood that the Italian Chambers and the ones abroad are two diverse realities, two parallel worlds. Until then, they had never really crossed paths, unless marginally. The former being national and more institutional. The latter with overseas rights and a more immediate entrepreneurial tilt. Naturally, I already knew of CCIE's (*Camere di Commercio Italiane all'Estero*) existence. Some are actually quite old, created at the end of the nineteenth century. But they had always acted as isolated units. Being in charge of the network of national Chambers put me in touch with the business communities created by Italians on the five continents. I thus touched upon the problems linked with globalization. It was the voices, the faces, the customs of thousands of men and women — especially, but not always, linked with the world of business and finance — those Italic features that appeared before my eyes, the ideal citizens of the global village. It was then I saw a potential to be exploited. An enormous potential, the dynamic force of a reality made up of communities found in every corner of the globe and that, though each different from the other, had many common character traits. More than intuition, it was a slow emergence of awareness. In those characters, I recognized obvious Italian traits, while realizing there was so much more to it. These communities were well aware of their original Italian roots, while knowing they now belonged to new homelands. There was a strong sense of today. A global spirit already in existence. And, above all, a need, a great desire to know themselves.

❖ *But at the time, you still had not come up with the terms* Italici *and* Italicity.

That is true. However, I have never liked the word "emigrant." I did not believe in it. Just as I felt that "Italian" no longer told the whole story.

❖ *Why not?*

Because by watching the children of the *Italian Diaspora*, who in the various countries had organized themselves into business communities—made up of both the original emigrants' descendants and the more recently expatriated managers or researchers—I immediately realized that they behaved more like stateless people than emigrants. What kept them together was not a passport or a flag, but a mentality, a style, a vision of the world: from the Americas to Australia. Drawn together by others who had chosen the same lifestyle. Not only a way of eating and dressing, but also behavior towards others, towards business dealings, to being drawn to and recognizing oneself in a certain type of art and culture, of sharing knowledge. It was then that I asked myself why, as Italians, we had not accepted this first challenge earlier by simply likening it to the historical story of Italian emigration. Why have we not ever been aware of the scope and economic potential of the "Italian nation in the world," a nation far greater than the one occupying the Italian peninsula?

❖ *A nation beyond the national borders and, what's more, created by a Diaspora. A somewhat difficult concept to sell. Not helped by the term—Diaspora—that was not immediately understood and caused you all kinds of problems.*

And yet I was proven right. Yes, *Diaspora* is a heavy word, packed with a sense of anguish. It can instill fear. But I used it only after a great deal of thought. *Diaspora* means dispersion, flight, and brings with it a deep sense of devastation. It starts with a departure, often tragic, from one's original homeland. But, as I pointed out some years later in a book in which my name was not officially featured,[1] I cannot imagine it by simply grasping this sense of loss. Instead, in the term Diaspora, I see something closer to the etymology of the word. In antique Greek, the verb *diasperein* literally means sew seeds, put down roots. Thus, it has connotations of development, of growth, of improvement, of future. Besides that, Italian is a Diaspora in a stronger sense. In other words: a transnational *polis* kept together by an unbreakable sense of *us*, which is recognized in both Italianity and business. I was convinced that the conditions existed to regroup the world created by this Diaspora via the cohesion of business. Or rather: Why not exploit the Diaspora to create a system of relationships and worthwhile economic and cultural contacts, and a lifestyle? I believed then, and still believe now, that the system that emerged would have been superior to the institutional networks of the various official overseas Italian centers due to the remarkable appeal of the *Made in Italy* brand.

❖ *It is the same idea that acts as a breeding ground for the so-called global communities. But they were considered little more than so-called ethnic groups: English-speaking, Hispanic, Chinese.*

Yes. When the concept of global communities began to make itself felt one imagined *populations* not divided by nationality, but by

---

[1] François Sauzey, *Anti-Prince, Poema Politica* (Anti-Prince, Political Poem), preface by Arrigo Levi, *The Flamingo*, Bologna, 1996. The author, at the time European functionary responsible for the Trilateral Commission Press Office, talked with a character identified as P-B, initials easily identifiable as those of Piero Bassetti.

economic, scientific, professional, or emotive interests; thus no longer on the basis of citizenship, but in the interests and morals of a world oriented toward progressive unification. But who knows why some think it has nothing to do with us. I, on the other hand, was and continue to be convinced that, on a par with *Hispanidad*, for example, and the other great ethnic movements of a local cohesion on a global scale, Italicity also has a strong capacity to aggregate. The difference between Hispanics and Italici is that the latter are unaware of their specificity and the potential wealth that can be gained from it. The numbers are all there, but they are not understood.

❖ *But are the numbers really there? Are you sure? Are we sure that the* Italian system *can still function as a driving force or as a model to the Italic system? Abroad, myriad articles and statements exaggerate Italy's economic, political, social, cultural decline. We're even accused of lacking happiness.*

I do not agree there's a decline. And I insist the question makes no sense. For the simple reason that, in a world order fast becoming more global—or rather glocal—where the old borders are crumbling, it does not make sense to measure the competitiveness and the vitality of a system by restricting it to the old borders. If Italy really were declining as a country, there's nothing to show that decline had anything to do with the Italicity system. In this way, for example, the so-called *brain drain* that everyone worried about, if taken from an Italici point of view, should in reality be seen as an investment. This is what the British Commonwealth understood right from the start. The British engineer or teacher or artisan, by going to work in India—to earn a salary—did not weaken London; on the contrary, he *enriched* the Commonwealth. Another example, though not quite the same, reaches a similar conclusion: over thirty percent of Italians living in Northern Italy earn a salary per capita higher than the European average. They too *enrich* the Italic Commonwealth.

❖ *It is evident that this concept of Italicity looks to the* future, *way ahead of anyone else, when compared to the simpler way in which one usually confronts the question of Italian emigration.*

That is what the centralist politicians have failed to understand. In the same way they refused to accept the concept of *Diaspora*. That, in some way, blamed them and the previous generations of political leaders, who were all highly distracted—for want of a better word—when it came to dealing with the Italians who had left Italy. For the same psychological reason, they turned their backs on the latter who were directly involved. They complained, and who can blame them, of the old country's lack of interest in them, while having no idea that they had become the new active guinea pigs of a project, of *another* far bigger nation. Today, things are beginning to change. One realizes, as mentioned by Fabio Porta, UIM's (Unione degli Italiani nel Mondo — Union of Italians in the World) coordinator for South America, that the Italic system even if it cannot depend on raw materials or energy sources "boasts a gasoline that no one else has: the great community of Italians abroad." Porta adds something that I agree with: "The day in which the chapter 'Italians abroad' is transferred from 'expenses' to 'investments', we will witness a complete reversal in the trends and values of a unique ability to integrate in distant and diverse countries."[2] This seems to be an important step forward, if who said this is an exponent of what many continue to call simple emigration and is, instead, Diaspora from whose humus the Italic network is born. On top of that, with regards to the accusations of the decline we talked of before, Porta asks,

---

[2] Interview at NIP, *News Italia Press*, January 8. 2008.

somewhat provocatively: "What if the future of Italy depended on we Italians living abroad?" As you can see, a new awareness is making inroads into the psyche of the Italic players. Anyway, it is immediately clear to me that having learned through the centuries to live in our own land with people from across the Alps and beyond the seas who came here to command, the people who left the "Boot" in search of a better life took the experience with them and elaborated a specific culture. That allowed them to maintain their own regional identity, to cultivate art and concentrate on the quality of life. Even when they had to change laws and customs: both those of their new homeland and of the old homeland they had just left. A philosophy of life to which millions of Italians have contributed, Italians who have learned to live with other cultures by emigrating or expatriating, spreading the seed of a profoundly humane and increasingly fashionable way of life.

❖ *And you think that through the overseas Italian Chambers of Commerce one can initiate something new? Is this how the association of overseas Chambers was born?*

Yes, in March 1987. I took advantage of the first article of the Chambers' statute that, at the time, foresaw a "section of the Italian Chambers of Commerce abroad." That was its first name. This new association was formally given life by seven chairmen of CCIE. It did not include a single member or institute of the Chambers of Commerce. The first chairmen were chosen in their field: Mario Gasperi, chairman of the Chamber of Frankfurt from 1987 to 1990. Mario Donn, the Chamber of Paris until 1993. I did not want people who were already at the CCIE—rightfully jealous of their very own independence and local identity—to feel in any way that they were being colonized by an Italian "center." In fact, it was common knowledge that on average the number of members per Chamber were: thirty percent of Italian companies (branches or local satellites of small and large public or private businesses), forty percent of foreign companies interested in doing business with companies in Italy or within the Italian–overseas circuit, and the remaining thirty percent a mixture of companies.

❖ So *the majority was not really Italian.*

Exactly. So, if one wished to accept the closeness of the Italian–overseas Chamber system to the interests closer to those strictly Italian, one needed to fully grasp what the exact nature of this *tertium genus* actually was. It was and remains the entire mechanism's pointer of the scales.

❖ *Tertium genus? Meaning? What are the characteristics of this new entity?*

It is something we saw immediately. It emerged the moment we started to organize the conventions that, at least once a year, bring the overseas Chambers together with their Italian counterparts. The differences are obvious. Made up of many things: from the foreign nationalities of many of the chairmen and secretaries, to the difficulties many of the delegates had speaking Italian, from the constant reminders of their origins to a different way of handling business and their modus operandi. It was a totally different mentality with respect to the Italian one. One of their first and constant appeals was for greater consideration concerning their diversity with respect to the other organizations recognized by the Italian state present in the foreign cities and nations where they operated: embassies' commercial attaches, consulates, ICE (*Istituto del Commercio Estero* — Institutes of Foreign Commerce) offices, the regions' economic representatives, the Italian Manufacturers' Association. But also, at a different level, the Italian Cultural Institutes, RAI TV International, etc. All *national* entities with a comprehensible tendency to operate according to strictly Italian methods. Methods I define as *radial*, in other words always originating from an exclusively Italian center: Rome, Milan, etc. And always answerable to them. A spider web with a spider at its center.

❖ *You must admit that is a harsh comparison. Another of your comparisons that not everyone understood immediately. You maintain that the central and phagocytic spider must be eliminated. That it should be scaled down, or at least its* Italian Italian *influence based more on the* Overseas Italy. *But how could one invent a new system of relations between these two Italys?*

By creating a more reticulate system. But no more centric. The so-called *foreign* Chambers have not released even so much as a scrap of a report, separate or otherwise, recognizable by a unit run by the Italian spider. The overall picture was very different. Unknown to them, the CCIE, including the Chambers not in contact with each other, were already a complex and unitary global business community, a real and significant network involving companies situated all over the world. However, their objective was not necessarily in line with the Italian one; their relations developed via the network, connected to the other junctions of the same network, but without necessarily going through Italy. Let us imagine that if the associate entrepreneur at the Buenos Aires Chamber of Commerce or his chairman, for his own requirements, needed a contact in Caracas or Sydney, he would not do it through Italy. He would not ask the Italian institute for *permission* or for help: he would take care of it himself. In short, the network was polycentric.

❖ *And on the basis of these conditions, did the Association of Overseas Chambers succeed in growing?*

In no time at all, the CCIE world grew up to around forty

Chambers of Commerce. And when, in November of '99, I resigned the chairmanship of the Association of Overseas Chambers, the CCIE associates numbered sixty-two in thirty-nine countries. Today, they are present in forty-eight countries with one hundred forty offices, and over twenty-three thousand associate companies, of which about seventy percent are local businesses — therefore non-Italian — that operate or are interested in working with Italy and with companies that, though not Italian, are part of the circuit. Among other things, there was a strong upsurge in Asia where initially there were only two Chambers; now there are seven. And not only in a decisive market like China's in which I had gambled immediately. Development in Europe was also very strong. And in Eastern Europe, where they did not exist initially, they can now boast a network that includes Budapest, Prague, Bratislava, Bucharest, Sofia, and Moscow.

❖ *Let us go back to the misgivings. Did they not seem natural to you? And the suspicions, the fears of being abused? The jealousies of one's own local independence? The defense of the idea of being subject to a constitutional state that is not Italian? Was there not any intelligible resistance?*

In some ways, yes. But I was certain I could rise above them. Starting from the bottom. Aggregation could only take place from the bottom up. On one side the central structure in Italy, the overseas Italian Chambers of Commerce, was intentionally very light: made up of very few people, its bureaucracy reduced to a minimum. In order not to *frighten*, and to really be a practical point of contact with Italy for the operators who lived abroad, the device had to be useful, but not binding, for comparisons with the offices, ministries, legal and commercial practices that were necessary for dealing with the respective affairs. And then cautiously we started — and always with the same non-invasive and non-binding spirit — to build a network.

❖ *But how can you build a network if the actual* players *are unaware of being part of it, and not readily open to the idea of already being within a network, its transnational dimensions capable of instilling fear?*

By choosing, once again, to aim for the minimum common denominator. In this case: information and communication. We'll have CCIE carry out a census of the newspapers and the 'Italian' radio and television transmissions present in their countries. The Italian institutions showed interest in the project. When they saw us at work, determined and already up and running, the Italian Foreign Affairs Ministry and the Presidency sponsored us partially. What emerged was a surprising cataloguing of that varied, detailed, and unknown universe represented by the Italian media abroad: a network made up of tiny realities, but, in its entirety, vast and well entrenched in its respective countries.[3] On top of that we used the formidable instruments that technology had to offer us. And so, respecting the individual autonomies, aware we were dealing with foreign companies, and local rights, we began to add the overseas Chambers to the network. Today — logging on to www.assocamerestero.com — it is possible to reach them all, to contact each single association, plus the companies and the operators associated with them.

❖ *You stress respect for autonomies. While, at the same time, you say you are convinced of the existence, the potential at least, of an* adhesive *that gives life and binds a global network still to be completed. How can these two extremes be compatible?*

I'll give you an example. Years after the first study of the Italian media abroad, a second, more in-depth study was carried out.

---

[3] Niccolò d'Aquino, *I media della diaspora.*

That, amongst other things, tried for the first time to take a census not only of the media, but also the *communicators* ascribable to Italicity.[4] Apart from the quite surprising results—over 1,500 communicators at the first count: a potential to be exploited, something I believe everyone understands, everyone, that is, except Italian politicians—I was amazed by the diversity of the response. In Latin America, particularly in Argentina, the study was made simpler by the great attachment to one's origins, typical of the *Italian* communities of that area. Whereas, in North America and Europe the distinct importance given to privacy and, at the same time, the ease with which the immigrants' have integrated with the local societies are partly to blame for the difficulty in putting together any relevant data. And yet we have respected this diversity. We have in no way forced our hand.

❖ *However, a project is an idea that wants to become something concrete and to do so must first become a fulfilled thought before being discussed publicly. A revolutionary idea requires a* manifesto.

Certainly. It requires elaboration. A thought spoken aloud. This was immediately clear. There were at least two of these moments right from the word go. Other *manifestos* followed. But the first two kicked off the process. In 1993, *Impresa e Stato* (Business and State), the Milan Chamber of Commerce's magazine, published a practically monographic edition on the Italian business communities around the world, about the possibilities of reshaping the country through a common project on the Roman Diaspora.[5] The immediate result was the real *manifesto*, as you call it. We commissioned two Roman sociologists, Consuelo Corradi and Enrico Pozzi, to carry out a study that was published under

---

[4] *Annuario dei Communicatori Italici nel Mondo* (Yearbook of Italic Communicators in the World). Turin: MediaPress, 2004.
[5] *Impresa e Stato* (Business and State), 22, 1993.

the title *Il Mondo in Italiano* (The World in Italian).[6] It was the first essay on processing and analyzing the ways and methods according to which we began to organize, or rather were already organized. The Italian communities beyond the Italian borders. A highly detailed enquiry that, examining certain paradigmatic cases in some of the more numerous and economically active communities, in North America, Argentina and Brazil, told us they were not just looking for an opening to do business with Italy or with businesses interested in their Italo-local products.

❖ *What were they looking for?*

They had set their sights on their identity as *mixed communities* being recognized among local businesses that were not necessarily of Italian origin. Certain curious facts emerged. For example, the major part of the Italian entrepreneurs abroad have declared their mistrust of Italy and its institutions: especially the commercial ones, but also political and institutional. This had become quite clear to us. However, the same mistrust was also expressed with regard to the other Italo-foreigners. Many declared that they were in business with local partners, who had nothing at all to do with Italy. So the two researchers had a great idea. Guaranteeing confidentially, they asked some of them for permission to see their respective address books and work notes. They also asked if they could watch them at work for a week, in silence, again promising absolute secrecy. They discovered what they had suspected. That, in reality, though they denied it — in good faith, naturally — the Italian entrepreneurs traded with, did business with, and, above

---

[6] Consuelo Corrado, Enrico Pozzi, *Il Mondo in Italiano. Gli Italiani nel Mondo, tra Diaspora, Business Community e Nazione* (The World in Italian. The Italians in the World, Between Diaspora, Business Community and Nation), preface by Piero Bassetti, I Quaderni di Impresa e Stato (The Exercise books of Business and State). Milan: Milan's Chamber of Commerce, 1995.

all, negotiated with their *similars*. When, at the end of the week, this was pointed out to them, they were stunned.

❖ *So, though not acknowledged, the network already existed in one form or another.*

Yes. And it was not limited to the amount of radial bilateral rapports, their content hybrid Italo-foreign, as originally thought. Instead, it turned out to be widely spread throughout the copious mass of working *metanational* relations in which it was organically immersed. For example, while Italian business looked to the CCIE purely as a place where to meet other businesses, a foreign company being placed there with a radial outlook—every now and then, the spider moved to the outer edges of the web in search of food—the local foreign company did not go to its home Chamber of Commerce only to meet visiting Italian companies. It also went to meet a world of local companies, whose only affinity with Italy was in how they did business, despite not being exactly *Italian*, its origins rooted in the local civil and economic fabric. It was then we began to think that the system was also made up of Italian-speaking people without an Italian passport: Ticinese, Dalmatic, Sammarinese, or Maltese. It was the next step, one that we would work on at a later date.

❖ *So once the overseas Chamber project was underway, you moved on to other things? Are you talking about Italicity?*

The natural step after reflections on the *World in Italian* was to produce a neologism: Italici. Anticipating your next question, I believe that in this case the ideological *manifesto* might have been an article that I wrote in 1998 for the geopolitical magazine *Limes*.[7]

---

[7] Piero Bassetti, "Il mondo in italiano," *Limes* 4 (1998).

It talked of a "network society in which the Italian nature is one of aggregation and recognition" singling it out as "a virtual community, not modeled on traditional criteria of identification and *belongingness*; capable, however, of gradually gaining strength enough to open up and make itself available to new and continuous adhesions from abroad, to establish a network of well connected poles, despite lacking territorial continuity." I wrote "an immense container of values, of ideas, of cultures and experiences represented by that collection of people, interests, relations, by that latent community or *polis* that live beyond the borders of Italy, but look at Italicity as an element of aggregation." I declared myself convinced that "for these new people, Italicity — meant not as citizenship, but as a system of values — may turn out to be an important strategic resource."

❖ *To put it more simply, even the Americans or the Germans, who do not have a drop of Italian blood in their veins, but prefer Italian products and that certain Italian way of life — from the Ferrari to Chianti wines, to Italian clothing, to living as much as possible in Italy — may be considered Italici.*

To put it simply, yes.

❖ *Once again, these are difficult concepts for people to accept. There were protests . . .*

And how! We went from mistrust of the word's validity — the term *Italicity* was not considered different to *Italianity* — to the idea that Italian experiences of emigration could not be and should not be comparable to those of the Ticinese, the Sammarinese, or the Dalmatians. It seemed quite odd. Then we had the lexical problem, but with psychological implications — historically speaking, the Italici were the various populations of the peninsula that the Romans gradually took under their wing, with or without force. But most of the resistance was political. It seemed politically blasphemous that, as implicated in our reckoning, the *Italic community* could unite people considered so different: the Italians of Italy, Italians abroad, citizens of Italian origin, but with different passports and — heaven forbid! — Italian-speaking people like the Ticinese, the Dalmatians and the Sammarinese.

❖ *What was the basic objection?*

That the task, which until then had been taken for granted, would complicate itself. In other words, that every summons to traditional loyalties of birth would impede that separation, forcibly uphold the old passport, maintain allegiance to the Italian central institutions. Including their foreign branches. For example, one of the feared implications — a minor one, but not to be underestimated — was that organizations like the CGIE (*Consigli Generali degli Italiani all'Estero* — General Council of Italians Abroad) would be superseded. Though established in the various countries, they bow — economically as well — to the Farnesina, the Italian Ministry of Foreign Affairs. They are like small centers of power, and treated as such.

❖ *So you were messing with consolidated interests.*

What is difficult to explain to those who have these suspicions is that we do not believe the Italian state should become a hypothetical Italici state. The concept of Italicity is not an extension of State, or of *statuality*. Thus, the frontier and laboratory of Italicity is a new ethnicity based on belonging rather than nation, open to different experiences and traditions. Thus: multiple.[8]

---

[8] Piero Bassetti, *Non più Immigrati ma Italici* (No Longer Immigrants but Italici), afterword by Otto Bitjoka, Marina Gersony, *Ci siamo. Il futuro dell'immigrazione in*

❖ A belonging *that includes the so-called Generation Two or G2, meaning the offspring of foreign immigrants in Italy. The young, who were born here or raised here, are also Italici, right?*

And how! A recent survey by the Agnelli Foundation shows they now number one million. Italian is their mother tongue, complete with the local accents of where they live — Milan, Rome, Palermo, etc. They speak it at school, with their friends. While at home with their parents, they perhaps speak in the language of the country they originally came from. But what matters is that they *think* in Italian. And write in Italian. A recent census catalogued over two hundred fully fledged writers, male and female, already belonging to this category. Perhaps meaning to provoke some kind of reaction, the English scholar John Foot, when talking of football, a significant phenomenon as far as we are concerned, suggests that the Italian football team at the 2018 World Cup will be made up of mixed races. And yet, Italian governments continue not to grant citizenship to this generation of new Italians. Italian politics, with some exceptions, continues not to understand that the passage from an idea of nationality implicitly based upon a presumption of the population's relative homogeneity to a pluralistic and negotiated conception of national belonging — where what counts is not only blood but also socialization, prolonged residency and the will to adhere to the pact of citizenship — will be the critical point of constructing a national identity capable of incorporating the second Italian generation.[9]

Italia (Here we go. The Future of Immigration in Italy). Milan: Sperling & Kupfer, 2007.
[9] Maurizio Ambrosini, "Il futuro in mezzo a noi: le seconde generazioni scaturite dall'Immigrazione nella società italiana dei prossimi anni" (The Future In Our Midst: the Second Generations Born from Immigration into the Italian Society in the Coming Years), speech made at the convention "A Future for Immigration in

Instead, the G2s continue to be looked upon as foreigners and thus not officially integrated until their eighteenth birthday, when they are supposed to return to their parents' country of origin and request permission to go back to Italy from there.

❖ *This helps create misfits and potential elements of trouble and malaise for society.*

Exactly. Look at what is happening in the French *banlieue*. Rightly so, the G2s refuse to accept that their integration comes with the same price of inferiority that their fathers suffered, that the taciturn acceptance of immigration is based upon the premise of it being provisional.[10] The challenge is in trying to understand that these second generations are in reality a huge opportunity, an important new source of energy and vitality for the social systems, like the Italian one which, economically and demographically, could do with a serious boost.[11] France, Germany, and the United Kingdom have understood this and — in spite of the fact that they are also guilty of errors and discrimination — have a more far-reaching approach than Italy that, when it comes to increasing the population, is shortsighted to say the least. With negative political consequences also at a European level: the recent reduction of seats at the European Parliament at Strasburg to make room for the new community members did not affect Paris, Berlin or London. The low birth rate in France, Germany, and the United Kingdom is *compensated* by new arrivals from the most diverse

---

Italy: the Outlook of the Second Generations." The Giovanni Agnelli Foundation, Turin, June 10, 2003.

[10] *Ibid.*

[11] Marco Demarie, "L'integrazione delle seconde generazioni: uno Sguardo al futuro italiano" (Integration of the Second Generations: A Look at the Italian Future), speech made at the convention "Foreigners' Children or No One's Children? Minor Immigrants, European Protagonists of Today and Tomorrow," The Giovanni Agnelli Foundation, Loreto, July 28, 2005.

countries, who have been given citizenship and passports. In Italy, no one appears to understand that the position of the G2s is a transitional phenomenon between an already maturing international order—and thus destined to evolve into something else—and the new glocalist order. An increasingly more mobile world cannot retreat behind a sterile system of national and geographic belongingness that everything shows has been superseded. With Globus et Locus, we propose to explain this, too. With the awareness that we will no doubt encounter new confrontations and suspicions.

❖ *How do you propose to explain it?*

Globus et Locus was born because I thought more of us should be made aware of the problem. We needed to show that the intuition that emerged at the economic and commercial level, and within the business community, could be enlarged to include the political community. And so, together with this concept and with the aim of furthering the research of problematic *glocals* rising from the dialectic between global and local, Globus et Locus was born in Milan in 1997. It is an association of diverse institutions, brought together by being bearers of functional interests in a glocal context: Chambers of Commerce, Regions, Foundations of banking origins, Universities, Communes, Provinces. On the one hand, the Association works as a research machine and, on the other, as a planning entity, offering a contribution to the activities of its members and to other national and international institutions with which it collaborates.

❖ *What do you propose with an organization like Globus et Locus?*

In the Globus et Locus book the term *local* indicates the vast geographic area of Northern Italy (from Piedmont to Friuli, down to

Tuscany, and including the Swiss Ticino)—meaning a geopolitical unit that forms one of Europe's richest and most developed macro regions. While the term *global* refers to the new context that sees the passage from an organized world on the basis of international relations to a new unitary vision. The nature of Globus et Locus' membership comes from these objectives, that includes representation of Northern Italy, stretching into Switzerland.

❖ *But is it not limiting geographically? Should it not include Central and Southern Italy that had, and still have, a lot to do with the* World in Italian?

We had to start somewhere. There was nothing limiting about our logic; it was rather effective. And it certainly is not closed to expansion. On the contrary! Our motto is: "Italici of the world unite!" By the way, the first modern Italic was Marco Polo. But if those like him and Christopher Columbus, the first Venetian, the second Genoese, took us to distant worlds, in a lesser way so did all the other Italians who established themselves around the globe. Every nation has had its explorers and ex-patriots, but few took with them the spirit of those great explorers. A "lofty" and refined civilization, however, that as a consequence of its own high cultural and democratic level inevitably made Italians mediocre colonizers. But, by the same grace, foreign thinkers and artists chose to adopt Italy, and be her offspring. Goethe, perhaps the most illustrious of them all, was in his own way an Italic. It is for this reason that we are working with Globus et Locus to highlight the development of diverse scientific and cultural in-depth studies. We have, for example, initiated relations with institutions and organizations like Società Dante Alighieri, the Catholic University of Washington, the Università IULM, and the Comunità Radiotelevisiva Italofona. The latter is a network, born about twenty years ago from the institutional collaboration between RAI, RTSI, RTV Ko-per-Capodistria, Vatican Radio and San Marino RTV that, under the leadership of Remigio Ratti, has proved itself in exploiting the Italian language and Italicity.

❖ *We are talking about an association whose main task is to spread and teach Italian around the world. Which raises a fundamental question. How can Italian – the language of a minority – hope to compete with English, today's Esperanto language?*

The real condition of the Italici spread across Europe and the world is one of generations who no longer speak Italian, or speak it badly. In the beginning, many of the immigrants spoke only the dialect of the region they had come from – Sicilian, Piedmontese, Venetian, etc. Someone counted the number of known dialects and, to his astonishment, found out there were thirty-one! Which tells the institutions, the Ministry of Foreign Affairs in particular, that we should not be stubborn about the Italian language; it was one of the first problems we had to overcome. Many of the first Diaspora media that we assessed back in 1994, especially radio and television, but also the printed word, used the local language, despite being aimed at the Italian community. Some even used their original regional dialect along with the local language. We were thus convinced, more so today than ever before, that to choose the *destination* language was even more appropriate. And perhaps, within the community circle, even more in line with a genuine European spirit. The European Union has over twenty members who want their national languages to be treated with respect. But everyone knows that in Brussels – very much a French-speaking city – the official language is English.

❖ *However, language is perhaps the most unifying element there is, giving a sense of country, of belonging. Are we supposed to give up Italian?*

On the contrary. To answer your question, I will refer to the Peace of Westphalia in 1648, that—I never tire of repeating—marks a decisive moment in history. The cardinal point of that treaty that governed Europe throughout the following centuries was *Cuius regio, eius religio*.[12] But there was also another: *Cuius regio, eius lingua*. The idea of collusion between language and power was affirmed. This idea has since been superseded, and should be queried. From this point of view, Switzerland acts in an exemplary manner. I feel that the Swiss have made the introduction of English into their schools a very serious debate. The risk of downgrading their confederate languages was a political risk not to be underestimated. Nonetheless, they have not rejected the language of global use: English.

❖ *And yet the Italian government has made it a point of honor to defend the use of Italian in its official documents within the European Union . . .*

Let me tell you a story. One day, a high-ranking French official addressed me in perfect English: "Mister Bassetti, you speak French, do not you? So speak to me in French, not English." And I

---

[12] *Cuius Regio, Eius Religio* (To whom the region {belongs}, his {is} the religion). This Latin expression had great significance during the period of Protestant reform and the successive centuries. It indicates an obligation on the part of the citizen to conform to the religion of the State's ruler, whether Protestant or Catholic. The idea of a State religion commonly refers to seventeenth- and eighteenth-century European history. It was used in the treaty following the Peace of Augsburg (also called the Religion of Peace) in 1555 between the emperor of the Holy Roman Empire, Charles V, and the forces of the League of Smalcalda to determine the Empire's religion as a co-existence between Lutheranism and Catholicism. The principal ratified at Augsburg signified that the rulers and the free cities were free to introduce the Lutheran faith (*jus reformandi*) and the same rights of the Catholic States in the Holy Roman Empire. Those of a different faith had to adapt to the State religion or emigrate. There also existed the version *Cuius regio, eius et religio*; in this case, the word *et* (meaning: and) has a strengthening function. In a word, it means "also."

did. But, I did so with the most profound contempt. If someone had told me that the official was defending the French language, I'd say he was wrong. In my opinion, he was causing only damage. The French language, defended in this way, has no future. By not defending itself, the Italian language shows it has a better future than French. Because it will progress further by following the line of non-resistance. It is not a policy of power, but one of conviction and practical use, one that has its own particular niches. According to statistics, it is no accident that Italian, other than English, is becoming one of the most taught languages in language schools around the world. This is a matter of choice, not of imposition, one of pleasure or professional necessity. Another episode comes to mind. Some time ago I happened to watch an angry exchange on television between two auto racing champions. Neither one was Italian. And yet, picked up by live microphones, they were both cursing each other in Italian, a language they both spoke quite well. And while we're at it, let me bring something else to your attention, this too has to do with that powerful and popular instrument called television. Have you noticed how the term "Italici" — not in the way we intend in this interview — pops up in shows and advertising? I remember, for example, a commercial for a well-known Italian beer.

❖ *The right to vote for Italians living abroad, reached after years of controversy, is a first response of the* Roman *political system from a global or even glocal point of view. How does it fare in the Italicity network?*

It does not. Yes, it has an impact on the constitutional set-up and on governmental and parliamentary stability, as we have seen. However, the way in which it has been drawn up produces more problems than solutions. Once again, the basic error is an old, almost Victorian vision of Italian politics. While the business community works to expand the Italic market place, and the civil society works to expand competitiveness and greater productivity, Parliament, defensively or myopically, tends towards restriction and refers everything to Rome. On top of that, the overseas vote also creates problems at an international level. Because the *invented* mechanism is particularly irregular. We have gone from forbidding Italians living abroad from voting to being the only ones who allow people of Italian extract to vote alongside the Italians. The result is that certain countries with a strong Italian immigrant population—major nations like the USA, Canada, Australia—have already let it be known that they will no longer tolerate *foreign* elections on their soil. The first such election was allowed, but never again. In practice, this creates a problem of citizenship and loyalty. Some Italians living abroad have dual-citizenship. They could find themselves in serious trouble if, with their vote, they contributed to decisions in conflict or not appreciated by the governments of the countries they have moved to or where they work. And I hate to think what might happen in the event of war. And let's face it, the "job" of these new members of the Italian Parliament—Congressmen and Senators—is not so much political, but—rightfully—to act as a lobby in favor of the respective communities of provenance. Many of which—another underlying question—see the vote as a means to gain Italian citizenship and an Italian passport. Not so much as a means back to Italy, but as a way into Europe. The Italo-Argentine, for example, once he has acquired European Union status thanks to the Italian passport, is more likely to move to Spain due more to the language than any employment advantages. In other words, someone messed up. In fact, steps are being taken to correct this problem.

❖ *First Diaspora, then Italicity. Recently, you suggested an even newer concept: an Italian Commonwealth. The word commonwealth immediately makes one think of the great British one. Is not it a rash comparison?*

I even mentioned it in my welcome speech to the Queen of England during her recent visit to Milan. In other words, to someone who understands the true meaning of commonwealth. I compared the Italici global community to a commonwealth of culture, experience, ideals, striving to create a communion with all the people who have Italian roots or can appreciate, like the great English landscape artist Joseph Mallord Turner, her history, her culture or, quite simply, that way of being open and friendly that distinguishes her. Turner, coming to Italy, painting her, showing her off, was a true and emphatic cultural ambassador. Not of a country, but of an idea that we today call Italicity. Or rather: everything that concerns Italy from a spiritual, tasteful and characteristic point of view. The differences with the British experience are obvious: from the political and power dimensions exercised in the past by the Crown, and the fact that English remained the principal language, while for us the Italian language slowly changed and finally disappeared, to be replaced by the local one. But, having said this, the United Kingdom and Italy have much in common. Especially within the European community. Things that can be used to create a united, more solid Europe, because — with respect to other countries like France and Germany — they have a very real economic, commercial and cultural *escape route*: the very close relationship with their respective diasporas.

❖ *And now? What solid future does all this have?*

To promote the visibility of Italicity we have come up with two strategies. The first is a website for the Italici. It must become the communication channel with the world in Italian. By going through the web with its modern and constantly improving instruments, like Second Life for example, we want to collect the experiences of the vast Italic universe and probe it deeply, stimulating interests and collecting reactions on the morals that we put forward and identifying the points of Italic aggregation. The knowledge that through the web one can better reach the players—who constitute the world in Italian, born from the certainty of a flexible system of which players and subjects play a part, with or without their awareness. And it is born from the practically unlimited range of action of a formidable instrument like the Internet. If well administered, it can *talk to* and *give voice to* an audience diversified by nationality, language, profession and culture. Thus guaranteeing the degree of a-territoriality and empiricism that the global dimension imposes. And then, second strategy, there exists a togetherness of activities not based on the web. Or rather: the cultural, intellectual and political study of the Italic concept. Devoted on one side to creating the support literature for the analysis of the theme, and on the other to organizing and coordinating a *think tank*. This involves editorial initiatives, along with the creation of bibliographic references. And on top of that: the communicational initiatives oriented towards the creation of interactions and exchanges through the organization of committees who will reflect on the substance and inquiries on specific categories of *Italici*.

ITALICITY
THE NEW WORD ENTERS THE OFFICIAL LANGUAGE

JULY 3, 2000. In the document *The World in Italian — The Search for an Italici Koine*, the committee of entrepreneurs and *Pro Italica* academics gathered at Milan's Palazzo Affari ai Giureconsulti to sanction the change from *World in Italian* to the new version *Italicity*, to give a first formal definition of the Italic community and indicate how this may establish itself in the global and local worlds interconnected by the Internet.

"*Italicity* — as explained in the document — generates a sense of casual belonging, not stiffened by legal constraints, based on ways of being and relating to others . . . The binding factor isn't the language, the territory, the possession of a passport, the right to vote . . . All this matters of course, but what prevails is common sense and behaviour, how business is done, how associations are made, how a community becomes an integral part of the environment in which it has settled, despite being strongly linked to pre-emigration traditions . . . Being a part of the Italic community does not rule out being a part of the traditional local community . . . it is fun for anyone to enjoy a certain relationship with the rest of the world . . . The Italian presence in the world expresses itself through a series of relationships, be they economic, entrepreneurial or informative networks that are necessary to the global village. The two hundred and fifty million Italici . . . form a cross-border community ready to take on any political responsibility. Italicity's economic dimension is, perhaps, better equipped for a concrete declination than has actually been developed: think of the network of overseas Italian Chambers of Commerce, the expression and point of reference for the business community."

An Unexploited Communicative Network

In the sixty-one countries monitored in a scientifically calculated manner (*Annuario dei mass media Italici nel mondo*. Milan: MediaPress, 2003), the newspapers and the radio and television programs of the world's Italic network add up to six hundred seventy-nine. The same data have been confirmed in the Caritas–Migrantes *Report on the Italians in the World 2007*. Singularly, it deals with small communication businesses, if one excludes three newspapers: New York's *America Oggi*, Toronto's *Il Corriere Canadese* and Australia's *Il Globo*. But put together, they form a considerable network: well over one hundred million copies printed annually, about two hundred thousand hours of radio transmissions and, not counting Rai TV International, roughly thirty thousand hours of television.

Divided geographically, Europe—and how could it be otherwise—is in first place with two hundred sixty-seven newspapers. Next come Central and South America (214), North America (128), Oceania (34), Asia and the Middle East (20), Africa (16).

Taking it by single countries, the classification changes. In first place and way ahead of the other ten countries boasting Italicity means of communication is Argentina (104). Then we have: USA (65), Brazil (60), Canada (59), Switzerland (47), France (36), Australia (32), Germany (28), Belgium, United Kingdom and Uruguay (15).

The potential is massive. But, contrary to the other global communities, who understand that this type of media (especially TV) is fundamental in the widespread diffusion of their communications, the Italicity system continues to appear quite indifferent.

THE STAGES OF A WORK IN PROGRESS

The concept of *Italicity* took shape over time, starting in 1982 when Piero Bassetti joined the management of the Chambers of Commerce system, but more so during the period 1993–1997 when he went on to run the CCIE, the association of Italian Chambers of Commerce abroad.

The Italian communities abroad started a network. They understood they were no longer just ethnic groups distant from an original center but part of an active, vital, composite Diaspora, of a *world in Italian*. A transnational subject produced by the debate between global and local that prospered thanks to the success of the Italian economy and its model.

In 1994, a study by Enrico Pozzi and Consuelo Corradi, published a year later as *The World in Italian*, confirmed the existence of this phenomenon described as a *spontaneous polis*.

It was during those years, animated by the debate on voting rights for Italians living abroad, that the term *Italici* was first used, to which Globus et Locus has dedicated a project that is still a work in progress.

Formally implemented in July, 2000, in a document by the Committee of Pro Italic Entrepreneurs and Academics, the term became commonplace at the grand "Convention of Italians in the World" the following December, and was used frequently throughout the book *Globals and Locals* in 2001. The term was developed further in April 2002, in the opening speech of the "The Essence of Italian Culture and the Challenge of the Global Age" seminars organized in Washington by Globus et Locus and by the Catholic University of America, and polished in 2004 in the book *Italicity Identity in Pluralistic Contexts*.

THE ITALICI COMMUNICATORS IN THE WORLD

There are almost six hundred "communicators" — journalists, publishers, advertisers — in Argentina of Italian origin or who can be enrolled in some way or another into the checkered and still unexplored network of Italic communications. It is the most astonishing data to emerge from the first — and only — report on the subject. With Argentina, the researchers who kick-started the *Yearbook of Italic Communicators in the World* (MediaPress, Milan, 2003) have concentrated their attention, by their own admission, on a more accurate census with respect to the forty-nine countries examined. But the truly surprising result is the overall one. Even though the figures of the inquiry are incomplete — by defect — there emerges a reality of enormous and not yet fully exploited potential.

The total number of *Italic* communicators around the world number no less than fifteen hundred. Only a small part is made up of correspondents and contributors from the Italian media, while the sizeable majority, with local passports even though their surnames betray obvious Italian origins, operate for local associations and newspapers.

The partial classification is as follows:

- LATIN AMERICA: 960 operators in 13 countries. The leading ones are Argentina (595), Brazil (244), Uruguay (48), Venezuela (32).
- EUROPE: 236 operators in 22 countries. Leading are: Switzerland (49), Germany (42), France (36), United Kingdom (34), Belgium (17), Spain (16).
- NORTH AMERICA: 127 communicators in 2 countries: USA (66), Canada (61).

- OCEANIA: 60 communicators in 2 countries. Australia (58), New Zealand (2).
- ASIA and the MIDDLE EAST: 16 communicators in 6 countries. The leaders are: Israel (5), China (4), Turkey (3).
- AFRICA: 11 communicators in 4 countries. South Africa (6), Egypt and Tunisia (2), Kenya (1).

THE ITALIAN CONSTITUTION RECOGNIZES
"ITALIANS NOT BELONGING TO THE ITALIAN REPUBLIC"

At the root of the Italic concept there is a broader view of the Italian citizen (and there are not many of them) who is in some way ratified by the Constitution, giving "Italians not belonging to the Republic" who want to enter the civil service the same rights as those of Italian citizens.

In fact, Clause 2 of Article 51 affirms the principle of equal rights for every citizen, no matter condition and sex, emphasizing that "The law, for admission to public office and elective duty, may consider Italians not belonging to the Republic as having the same rights to citizenship."

Over the years, this principle has been amended to include other normative decrees. Here are some of the more significant ones.

The President of the Republic's decree of 03.05.1957, article 2, specifies that, among other things, to participate in the examination for employment in the civil service of the State, the candidates must declare: "a) date and place of birth; b) possession of Italian citizenship. Italians not belonging to the Republic have the same right to citizenship." The Rule of the examinations to enter the Senate's administrative structure, decreed by the Senate Chairman on 18.12.2002, in Article 3, states that "The proclamation of the examination may establish the general requisites of admission: a) Italian citizenship. Including those Italians not belonging to the Republic."

The Ministry of Education's decree of 21.06.2007, article 3, establishes the criteria for employment in the public schools, highlighting, in Clause 1: "From July 23, 2007, the candidates must have the following requisites: a) Italian citizenship (Italians not belonging to the Republic have the same right to citizenship) . . . "

Globus et Locus
A Study and Action Project

In this day and age, the debate on global and local provokes more questions than any other. Not to mention new populations like the Italici. Picking up on this connection, in the mid-nineties Piero Bassetti laid down the premises for a center to study the realities of glocal in its whole, the *Italicity* phenomenon and questions of a more immediate interest to Italy and its regions. Some entrepreneurs, politicians and academics responded in a positive way. And thus the Globus et Locus association was born, acting on the wishes of Milan's Chamber of Commerce and the Sacred Heart University, with the support of Turin's and Trieste's Chambers of Commerce, the Regions of Lombardy and Piedmont, the city of Lugano, the San Paolo Company and the Foundations of Cariplo and Turin's Cassa di Risparmio.

Amongst the initiatives embarked on by Globus et Locus, that aimed at turning ideas and reflections into strategic actions and in organizing and coordinating a sort of *think tank* alert to the glocal phenomenon, the Italici Project stands out. Apart from analyzing the phenomenon that unites all Italians, the descendants of emigrated or expatriated Italians, Sammarinese, Ticinese, Dalmatians and all the Italophiles, the project intends to favor the aggregation of the Italic community, especially through the Internet. The slogan "Italici of the world, unite" will be the catalyst to promote encounters and synergies between the leading players of the community. The network connections of Foundations, Regions, territorial associations, Chambers of Commerce, Universities, companies and all those who work to develop the territory and local communities, will also favor the link of the *Diaspora of local policies* with the regions of "the Boot."

ITALICI
EUROPEANS BORN FOR A GLOBAL COMMONWEALTH

The *Italicity* character emerges from a highly tormented history, marked by great political fragmentation and the various regions' horrendously unequal economic development, in a geographic context that made him a much sought after prey.

Huns, Arabs, Normans, Austrians, French, and Spanish: populations beyond our borders who have always craved the Italian peninsula, her possessions, and her culture. And have thus contributed to the evolution of an "open" local philosophy, enriched further by the discoveries of the great explorers like Marco Polo and Christopher Columbus and, in more recent times, by a migratory *Diaspora* that created *Little Italys* around the world before giving life to a principled and cultural commonwealth.

They are communities identifiable by their original culture, despite no longer speaking Italian, and over the past decades have absorbed managers and expatriated researchers in the most natural of ways. Each one feels Belgian, American, Argentine or Australian and wouldn't dream of giving up his or her new passport. However, they do remain attached to a common system of morals and customs that are being rediscovered. To a trait that fascinated foreigners down through the centuries. Like the English artist, Joseph Turner, whose paintings revealed to the world all the beauty and charm of Italy, who chose to become ambassador to its lands and not to a foreign State, inspired by its spirit, by its universal essence: by the Italicity character.

A character projected beyond the limits of the now declining States, open to supranational and transnational communities like the European Union. That in the new *Italico* will find the ideal, natural citizen. Born not of a national identity, but formed by a pluralist, universal and cosmopolitan civilization, far from any temptations of chauvinism.

WHO ARE THE ITALICI?
AN HISTORICAL IDEA THAT CROPS UP IN THE PRESENT

The term *Italici* once referred to the populations of the Italian peninsula who were defeated and herded together by the ancient Romans. Today, the term has taken on, or rather added on, a new significance: the Italic is a member of the vast network, or global aggregation, based on morals shared by a civilization to which the traditional Italic populations also contributed, but through the course of history — first Roman, then Christian, then Renaissance and finally today — has reworked itself in the post-modern key. A network that "makes" Italy, but characterizes territories like Italian Switzerland, Dalmatia, Istria, San Marino and Malta, touching on other countries such as Albania or Tunisia, first through cultural exchanges, followed by new bursts of immigration and the fundamental role of television imprinting. But it is a network that finds its real raison d'être in having put down roots in every corner of the globe: people, not only professionals, who appreciate a certain style and taste and that, perhaps without their being aware of it, reproduce that Italian way of life wherever they might be. Put all this together, and we are talking about a "new population" of roughly two hundred fifty million men and women. The "Italico" is a Post-Italian, a citizen of the world with a new identity. An identity that, based on regional origins more than national, flows between culture and a renewed interest in regional and ethnic characters.

The
Glocalist Manifesto

Piero Bassetti

Italian Publisher's Thoughts

Created and written by the regionalist and authentic federalist Piero Bassetti, the *Manifesto dei glocalisti* (The Glocalist Manifesto) is that *framework of the glocal profile* necessary to help understand and study an important and very actual theme like "Italicity." The individual's ever increasing mobility, the progressive resetting of the dimensions of time and space, the birth of new associations, the assertion of the global populations—like the Italic one—characterized by multicultures and multiorigins, are the characteristic signs of a post-modern era in which the values or advantage of relationships assume a growing importance: information, contact, shared identity.

If we now live in a glocal (simultaneously global and local) world, *The Glocalist Manifesto* is an initial conceptualization of great interest and will certainly contribute to the opening of the debate on the 'forms and forces' of the glocalized world.

Milan–Lugano, June 2008

We are glocalists

1. Because we know that technology, in changing our concept of time and space, has changed the world and made it one;
2. Because we know that in the world of knowledge, innovation is the moment in which knowledge and power come together to create custom, values and history;
3. Because we know that innovation means opportunity, yet can also constitute a threat;
4. Because we know that zero-time and zero-space mean the dominion of mobility over settlement;
5. Because we know that mobility means flows, networks and nodes of relationships independent of territory and its confines;
6. Because we know that relationships without boundaries change the meaning of place, bringing it closer to the meaning of node, opening up a new relationship between the global and the local, in which the global penetrates all *loci* through its networks, and each *locus* folds directly into the global;
7. Because we know that this new glocal world will be our world and our destiny.

But we are also aware

8. That glocalism must not mean stateless conformity, macdonaldization, imbalances or ecological disaster;
9. That to stem these threats new policies and institutions will increasingly be required;
10. That new policies and institutions mean new powers;

11. That recourse to legitimate force and territorial control will count less and less in a mobility-driven world;
12. That we do not need borders, citizenship, sovereignties or subordinate localisms to take advantage of the global while at the same time defending our local spaces;
13. That the end of nationalism does not have to mean the end of territorial ethnic cultural identities;
14. That in the global village the social movement will be protagonist;
15. That new political relationships must inform the management of mobility and territory;
16. That the enterprise constitutes the central form of mediation between coexistence and the economy;
17. That the enterprise is regulated by global markets;
18. That the populations of enterprises within these global markets operate on a global scale through logically interwoven networks of functions;
19. That these functions give rise to flows of goods, people and relationships that are relatively free of territorial considerations;
20. That traditional national and regional political institutions are increasingly hard pressed in influencing these relationships;
21. That only new glocal institutions, i.e. institutions capable of tying together global enterprises and local enterprise populations, are in a position to mediate between the global economy and local forms of coexistence;
22. That the crisis national states are currently undergoing in their capacity to regulate is in fact irreversible and that only profound institutional innovation can save us.

23. A new form of statehood in which diverse individuals, ethnicities and nations can coexist on equal terms, where territorial communities and communities of practice can interweave their interests and functions;
24. Networks and territories that are organized without nationalist or localist influences;
25. A new form of citizenship based on multiple affiliation;
26. The consequent ability to feel that we are cosmopolitan, Italics, Europeans, Mediterraneans, Northern Italians, Milanese, Catholics, Moslems, liberals, socialists, technical, humanists, Boca fans, Inter fans, etc., without losing our sense of political identity;
27. The ability to cultivate these new affiliations as individuals and as a community;
28. A new form of spatial laicism that protects the new mobility, in the knowledge that a life lived fully among a wealth of affiliations in multiple *loci* is far more authentic and richer than any form of monochord sectarianism;
29. The ability to operate freely within the rich and dynamic structure of functional and territorial networks the glocal world is preparing to offer us;
30. A new form of cosmopolitan governance, indispensable for protecting the environment, peace, human rights and justice in a glocal world.

TO ACHIEVE THIS, WE ARE PREPARED TO PUT ON THE LINE

31. Our current identities and political subjectivisms, in order to attain new structures of representation and governability;

32. Our traditional relationship to territory, in order to prepare ourselves for the influx of migrants that mass mobility will bring;
33. Our current local and national structures, which we will transform and adapt in order to meet the challenges that the demise of the nation–state and the advent of a glocal world will inexorably pose.

TO WORK TOWARDS THE ADVENT

34. Of the new thinking, the new parties, the new institutions and political practices that will have to take on the role of leaders and actors in the new glocal history;
35. Of the new aggregations that this path will need to subjectify;
36. Of the new relationships between settlements and mobility of things, people, and ideas;
37. Of rules for coexistence that reconcile efficiency and democracy in the new communities of practice and function on a global and local scale;
38. Of the urban reorganization driven by the springing up of glocal cities wherever intersections of functional networks and existing civic aggregations come together in new ways;
39. Of the new subnational political geography that regional aggregations are in the process of creating virtually everywhere;
40. Of the related institutions and their new powers;
41. Of the new levels of metanational statehood that are emerging throughout the world, beginning with Europe.

WE ARE LAUNCHING THIS APPEAL FROM MILAN

Because we are aware:

42. That Europe is the continent that invented the City;
43. That European unity will not be reconstructed by arranging its regional and metropolitan realities in forms imposed by the advent of the nation-state;
44. That the integration and rebalancing of the stronger and weaker areas of Europe will no longer be solely entrusted to the unifying power of the national states, but rather to the building of new interregional functional networks between areas that are not necessarily contiguous;
45. That, where Italy is concerned, its various parts will move within Europe in varied, complex ways, and it will witness the North, Center, South and Islands connect in new ways with the corresponding continental and global realities;
46. That, in these conditions, the glocal city in which we live and call Milania, being none other than a piece of the vaster dimension of Northern Italy and the Po valley, cannot reject its responsibility to connect the entire country with the rest of Europe.

THERE IS MUCH WORK TO BE DONE

47. In order to better understand, designate, organize, and institutionalize the great metropolitan area in which we live;
48. In order to mark out Milania's new if still uncertain identity;
49. In order to link this identity with the rest of Italy and Europe in a new way;
50. In order to allow new potentially glocal institutions like chambers of commerce, bank foundations, provinces, regions, and agencies to strengthen their connections with those

multinational companies, major banks and groups of SMEs already engaged in the glocalist challenge;

51. In order to enable the thousands of associations and service organizations animating Milania's local dimensions to learn to interconnect with the progressively denser web of functional networks that cross them on a glocal scale;

52. In order to stimulate our centers of cultural life to become more aware of the high rate of innovation that glocalization involves;

53. In order to bring efficiency and order to the myriad networks coursing through the glocal city, as well as to the thousands of enterprises that energize it and the forms of mobility that infuse it with life;

54. This is work in which we invite all those who share our ideas and aims to participate;

55. Because we need a better understanding of the realities in which we operate;

56. We must mobilize entire generations to meet the new challenges we clearly envision;

57. We must oversee the birth of new subjective realities capable of bringing political life to a new glocal world;

58. The Milanese must awaken to the new challenges of the glocal city in which they live;

59. Italic peoples the world over must come together in the awareness of an affiliation that transcends yet does not deny affiliations between Italians, or natives of Canton Ticino, Monte Titano or Dalmatian regions; and which unites with that affiliation any persons — be they Canadian, American, Latin American, Australian, or resident alien immigrants in Italy, etc. — who see themselves as Italic for reasons of origin, interest, culture or values;

60. Together we must begin to build the new institutions and new governance the glocal world needs;
61. In other words, we need a new glocalist policy.

And we hereby commit ourselves to work!

Milan, 7 January 2008

AUTHORS

PIERO BASSETTI, Milanese, is Chairman of Globus et Locus, the Association of Institutions that analyzes the consequences of glocalization on political and social life and on institutions, and of the Giannino Bassetti Foundation, its scope being the study of "responsibility in innovation." Advisor and councilor of the Comune of Milan from 1956 to 1967, he was the first President of the Lombardy Region from 1970 to 1974 and parliamentary deputy from 1976 to 1982; Chairman of Milan's Chamber of Commerce, Industry and Agriculture from 1982 to 1997, he was also Chairman of the Union of Italian Chambers of Commerce from 1983 to 1992 and of the Association of oversees Italian Chambers of Commerce from 1993 to 1999.

PAOLINO ACCOLLA, born in Sicily, was raised and studied in Milan. A professional journalist, he began his career in 1981 for monthly magazines that dealt with communications and science before moving abroad in 1984. He was the Far East correspondent for the press agency *Quotidiani Associati* and the daily newspaper *Reporter*; writer for the Italian language section of Radio Japan (NHK) in Tokyo; from 1987 to 2003, he was the ANSA correspondent in Tokyo, London, New York, Washington and Moscow. A freelance journalist once again, he worked for the press agency AdnKronos International, the *Corriere della Sera* and Radio 24 in Southern Asia. Back in Italy since 2006, he teaches journalism and writes articles on science and foreign affairs for various weeklies of the Espresso, RCS and Hachette groups. Over the past few years, he has also collaborated on various books for Gutenberg Publishers. In 1984, he published the collection of poems entitled *Blue Solo*. He speaks English and Spanish as second languages; as well as Chinese, French and Japanese.

NICCOLÒ D'AQUINO, journalist, was born in Italy and for a long time lived outside the country. He worked in Milan for *Il Giornale* run by Indro Montantelli and in the Principality of Monaco for the Italian network of Radio Montecarlo. For many years he was the correspondent for the ANSA press agency in New York, from where he contributed regularly for the daily Swiss *Il Corriere del Ticino* and for the Italian language Swiss radio. He returned to Italy to join the editorial staff of the financial weekly *Il Mondo*. Currently with the Rizzoli Group in Milan, he is the *Corriere della Sera* correspondent. He took part in the realization of *I media della diaspora: Newspapers, Radio and Television of Italy outside Italy* (Istituto Poligrafico e Zecca dello Stato, 1994), and with the successive *Annuario dei mass media e dei comunicatori italici nel mondo* (Media Press, 2004). He also contributed to the radio Encyclopedia (Garzanti, 2003), by writing the introductory piece *Le Radio nel Mondo.*

GLOBUS ET LOCUS

The Association was born in 1997, its objective being to analyze the glocal problems emerging from the dialectic between global and local.

The Association acts as a branch of learning, of research on one side and planning entity on the other, while offering a contribution to the activities of its members and other national and international institutions which collaborate with it.

The current members of Globus et Locus are:

- Milan's Chamber of Commerce
- Turin's Chamber of Commerce
- Trieste's Chamber of Commerce
- The Lombardy Unioncamere
- The San Paolo Company
- The Cariplo Foundation
- The Cassa di Risparmio Foundation of Turin
- Region of Lombardy
- Region of Piedmont
- Province of Piacenza
- Catholic University of the Sacred Heart
- City of Lugano

In the Globus et Locus book the term *local* indicates the vast geographic area of Northern Italy (from Piedmont to Friuli, down to Tuscany, and including Swiss Ticino) — meaning a geopolitical unit that forms one of Europe's richest and most developed macro regions. While the term 'global' refers to the new context that sees the passage from an organized world based on international relations to a new global vision.

There are three problematic principles at the center of Globus et Locus reflections and actions to do with the impact of globalization on:

- governance and institutions
- populations and civilized societies
- formation and political culture of reference
  for glocal players

Since 2007 Globus et Locus is accredited by the Economic and Social Council of the United Nations (ECOSOC) with Special Consultative Status.

Globus et Locus
Via Brisa, 3 – 20123 Milan, Italy
www.globusetlocus.org
info@globusetlocus.org

Some publications by GL:

- P. Bassetti, *Globals and Locals! Fears and Hopes of the Second Modernity*, by S. Roic. Milan-Lugano: Giampiero Casagrande Publisher, 2001, second printing 2003;
- *The Essence of Italian Culture and the Challenge of a Global Age*, Proceedings of the seminar convened April, 2002, at the Catholic University of America in Washington. Washington: The Council For Research in Values and Philosophy, 2002;
- *Italic Identity in Pluralistic Contexts, Toward the Development of Intercultural Competencies*, Proceedings of the seminar organized by Globus et Locus in April, 2003, at the Catholic University of America in Washington. Washington: The Council For Research in Values and Philosophy, 2004;
- AA.W., *Milan, centre of global network*. Milan: Bruno Mondadori, 2005;
- S. Roic (by), *Globus et Locus, The Route of Italicità*. Milan-Lugano: Giampiero Casagrande Publisher, 2006 (provisional edition);

- P. Accolla, N. d'Aquino (by), *Italici, The Possible Future of a Global Community*. Milan-Lugano: Giampiero Casagrande Publisher, 2008.

From the CFS (Casagrande-Fidia-Sapiens) catalog:

- *Carlo Cattaneo (1801–1869): An Swiss Italian*, Antonio Gili (2001);
- *Federalism. An Italian, Swiss, European Challenge*, (2002);
- *Regions in Europe, Constitutional Experiences by Comparison*, by Beniamino Caravita (2002);
- *Political Reflections, Institutions, Communications and Formation for Citizenship*, by Oscar Mazzoleni, (2003);
- Federalism and Devolution. The Swiss Experience and the New European Challenges, by Oscar Mazzoleni, (2003);
- *The Polytechnic of Carlo Cattaneo. The Editorial Happening, the Collaborators, the Ratings*, by Carlo G. Lacaita, Raffaella Gobbo, Enzo R. Laforgia, Marina Priano (2006);
- *Interpreting Switzerland, Origins and Becoming the Helvetic Model*, Remigio Ratti (2006);
- *New European Regions. The Challenges of Insubria, Como, Lecco, Novara, Canton Ticino, Varese, Verbano-Cusio-Ossola*, by Roger Friedrich, Sergej Roic, Antonio Franzi, Robi Ronza (2005).

NOTES

NOTES

VIA FOLIOS

*A refereed book series dedicated to Italian studies
and the culture of Italian Americans in North America*

GIOSE RIMANELLI
The Three-legged One
Vol. 54, Fiction, $15

CHARLES KLOPP
Bele Antiche Stòrie
Vol. 53, Criticism, $25

JOSEPH RECAPITO
Second Wave
Vol. 52, Poetry, $12

GARY MORMINO
Italians in Florida
Vol. 51, History, $15

GIANFRANCO ANGELUCCI
Federico F.
Vol. 50, Fiction, $15

ANTHONY VALERIO
The Little Sailor
Vol. 49, Memoir, $9

ROSS TALARICO
The Reptilian Interludes
Vol. 48, Poetry, $15

RACHEL GUIDO DE VRIES
Teeny Tiny Tino's Fishing Story
Vol. 47, Childrens, $6

EMANUEL DI PASQUALE
Writing Anew
Vol. 46, Poetry, $15

MARIA FAMÀ
Looking For Cover
Vol. 45, Poetry, $12

ANTHONY VALERIO
*Toni Cade Bambara's
One Sicilian Night*
Vol. 44, Poetry, $10

EMANUEL CARNEVALI
Dennis Barone, Ed.
Furnished Rooms
Vol. 43, Poetry, $14

BRENT ADKINS, et. al., Eds.
Shifting Borders, Negotiating Places
Vol. 42, Proceedings, $18

GEORGE GUIDA
Low Italian
Vol. 41, Poetry, $11

GARDAPHÉ, GIORDANO,
& TAMBURRI
Introducing Italian Americana
Vol. 40, ItalAmerStudies, $10

DANIELA GIOSEFFI
*Blood Autumn /
Autunno di sangue*
Vol. 39, Poetry, $15 / $25

FRED MISURELLA
Lies to Live by
Vol. 38, Stories, $15

STEVEN BELLUSCIO
Constructing a Bibliography
Vol. 37, Ital.Americana, $15

ANTHONY J. TAMBURRI, Ed.
Italian Cultural Studies 2002
Vol. 36, Essays, $18

BEA TUSIANI
con amore
Vol. 35, Memoir, $19

FLAVIA BRIZIO-SKOV, Ed.
*Reconstructing Societies
in the Aftermath of War*
Vol. 34, History, $30

TAMBURRI, et. al., Eds.
Italian Cultural Studies 2001
Vol. 33, Essays, $18

ELIZABETH G. MESSINA, Ed.
In Our Own Voices
Vol. 32, ItalAmerStudies, $25

STANISLAO G. PUGLIESE
Desperate Inscriptions
Vol. 31, History, $12

HOSTERT & TAMBURRI, Eds.
Screening Ethnicity
Vol. 30, ItalAmerCulture, $25

G. PARATI & B. LAWTON, Eds.
Italian Cultural Studies
Vol. 29, Essays, $18

HELEN BAROLINI
More Italian Hours
Vol. 28, Fiction, $16

FRANCO NASI, Ed.
Intorno alla Via Emilia
Vol. 27, Culture, $16

ARTHUR L. CLEMENTS
The Book of Madness & Love
Vol. 26, Poetry, $10

JOHN CASEY, et. al.
Imagining Humanity
Vol. 25, InterdiscStudies, $18

ROBERT LIMA
Sardinia / Sardegna
Vol. 24, Poetry, $10

DANIELA GIOSEFFI
Going On
Vol. 23, Poetry, $10

ROSS TALARICO
The Journey Home
Vol. 22, Poetry, $12

EMANUEL DI PASQUALE
The Silver Lake Love Poems
Vol. 21, Poetry, $7

JOSEPH TUSIANI
Ethnicity
Vol. 20, Poetry, $12

JENNIFER LAGIER
Second Class Citizen
Vol. 19, Poetry, $8

FELIX STEFANILE
The Country of Absence
Vol. 18, Poetry, $9

PHILIP CANNISTRARO
Blackshirts
Vol. 17, History, $12

LUIGI RUSTICHELLI, Ed.
Seminario sul racconto
Vol. 16, Narrativa, $10

LEWIS TURCO
Shaking the Family Tree
Vol. 15, Memoirs, $9

LUIGI RUSTICHELLI, Ed.
Seminario sulla drammaturgia
Vol. 14, Theater/Essays, $10

FRED GARDAPHÉ
Moustache Pete is Dead!
Long Live Moustache Pete!
Vol. 13, Oral Literature, $10

JONE GAILLARD CORSI
Il libretto d'autore, 1860–1930
Vol. 12, Criticism, $17

HELEN BAROLINI
Chiaroscuro: Essays of Identity
Vol. 11, Essays, $15

PICARAZZI & FEINSTEIN, Eds.
An African Harlequin in Milan
Vol. 10, Theater/Essays, $15

JOSEPH RICAPITO
Florentine Streets & Other Poems
Vol. 9, Poetry, $9

FRED MISURELLA
Short Time
Vol. 8, Novella, $7

NED CONDINI
Quartettsatz
Vol. 7, Poetry, $7

ANTHONY J. TAMBURRI, Ed.,
Fuori: Essays by Italian / American
Lesbians and Gays
Vol. 6, Essays, $10

ANTONIO GRAMSCI
P. Verdicchio, Trans. & Intro.
The Southern Question
Vol. 5, Social Criticism, $5

DANIELA GIOSEFFI
Word Wounds & Water Flowers
Vol. 4, Poetry, $8

WILEY FEINSTEIN
Humility's Deceit: Calvino Reading Ariosto
Reading Calvino
Vol. 3, Criticism, $10

PAOLO A. GIORDANO, Ed.
Joseph Tusiani: Poet, Translator,
Humanist
Vol. 2, Criticism, $25

ROBERT VISCUSI
Oration Upon the Most Recent
Death of Christopher Columbus
Vol. 1, Poetry, $3

Published by Bordighera, Inc., an independently owned not-for-profit scholarly organization that has no legal affiliation to the University of Florida, the John D. Calandra Italian American Institute, or State University of New York at Stony Brook.

www.ingramcontent.com/pod-product-compliance
Lightning Source LLC
Chambersburg PA
CBHW022126280326
41933CB00007B/560